THE LUNCHBOX NOTE

a story about loving others

Kristi Hayes &
Marianne Booth

ISBN: 978-1-61244-840-4
Library of Congress Control Number: 2020904526

Printed in the United States of America

Halo Publishing International
8000 W Interstate 10
Suite 600
San Antonio, Texas 78230
www.halopublishing.com
contact@halopublishing.com

Questions to discuss with your children after reading the book:

Do you know anyone at school like Holden?

How do you think Holden felt when Trevor didn't want to be his friend?

What does "be strong, protect the weak, love everyone" mean to you?

Where are some places that you can let your light shine?

Why is it important that we keep our eyes open to see those around us?

How can we love others well as a family?

Can you find all the hearts in each page?

be. love
zzz

The morning arrives. Sunlight shines golden.
Mom enters the room. "Good morning, Holden!"

It's the first day of school, filled with wonder and joy.
"I know you will love it," she says to her boy.

Holden thinks to himself as he puts on his clothes,
"Will today be a good one? No one quite knows.
So many new things. And who will I see?
No need to be nervous. I'm filled with glee!
I'll watch and I'll learn and I'll give it my best.
This first day of school will be my great quest!"

be.

Running down the stairs with a leap and a bound,
Holden is ready to conquer the town.
Breakfast is served: It's waffles. Hooray!
This is the best way to start off the day.

As he sits down, Holden sees a small note
in Mom's handwriting. He reads what she wrote:

"If you are nervous or a little bit scared,
we know you have worked and prayed and prepared.
Dad and I see that now is your time.
Go into the world and let your light shine!"

Mom starts to walk over to sit by his side.
Their smiles appear as fists gently collide.

Open your eyes to what others may need,
always be willing to guide and to lead.
Let your light shine as you move along.
Be who you are and help others be strong.

Now buckled in tight and ready to go,
"EYES WIDE, LIGHTS SHINE!" they chant down the road.

Holden keeps his eyes wide open and ready to see
how much of a gift to others he'll be.

It's time to walk in and meet some new friends.

Mom bends down to remind him again,
"EYES WIDE, LIGHTS SHINE," is all she can say.
With a hug she sends him on his way.

Walking inside, he says to himself,
"Let your light shine when others need help."

Holden walks in and sits down with some guys.
But then he spots Trevor with tears in his eyes.

Holden cares for Trevor's heart and doesn't want him to be sad.
He thinks, "Let my light shine. That should make him feel glad."

So, Holden walks over and gives a big smile and asks,
"Do you mind if I sit for a while?
Are you scared, are you worried, or just need a friend?
You can be friends with me, so your sadness may end."

And all through the day, Holden and Trevor have fun.
They don't even notice the setting sun.

When you let your light shine and make it grow brighter,
you put others first and make their loads lighter.

Snuggled in tight and ready for bed,
he whispers to Mom as she kisses his head:
"Today was a bright and special day.
Thank you for telling me to light someone's way."

"EYES WIDE, LIGHTS SHINE!" Mom cheers from the car as Holden jumps out, chasing friends near and far.

It's been a whole year and the words seem to stick.
Even the carpool lady thinks it's the trick!

On this new day, as he walks to the door,
he wonders what adventures are in store.

He runs up to play with his good buddy Trevor
but he didn't expect to be brushed off forever.

"Not today," says Trevor. He stands up from the floor.
"There's really no time for you anymore.
I've got some new friends that are funny and smart.
There's not enough room for you in my heart."

Holden tries hard to still be his friend
but he feels like their good times have come to an end.

That night at dinner, the family all chatters.
Mom looks at Holden and asks, "What's the matter?"

Holden starts to tear up as he tries to explain
how lonely he is, and the weight of his pain.

Early next morning, Dad knows what to do.
He'll give Holden some words, simple and true.

A small napkin-note for Holden to treasure;
something to bring him a small bit of pleasure.

Holden says to himself,
"Well, I can do that. I can be strong.
It doesn't matter if he did me wrong.
All I can do is hope and be kind.
Maybe one day I can change Trevor's mind."

Every morning, Holden waves and says, "Hi,"
but when Trevor ignores him, he doesn't cry.
The words from his dad echo deep in his heart:
Choosing love is the best place to start.

BE STRONG
Protect The Weak
Love Everyone
Be Strong, Protect the weak, Love everyone.
be.
chips

This small step in courage helps Holden to see
that loving others is the best way to be.
He talks to his parents and comes up with a plan
to keep spreading the love as far as he can.

He has an idea to help those who are sad.
He'll lean on those words written by Dad.
They gather supplies and put care bags together,
helping people without homes survive changes in weather.

It's just a small way to show others he cares
when what they're most used to is judgement and stares.

"Be strong," Holden thinks, "even when others hurt you.
Protect the weak even when you don't want to."

And, lastly, "Love everyone."
That's the key to it all
because it's our job to make others feel tall.

Be
Strong, Protect
the weak, Love
everyone.
chips
be.

CPSIA information can be obtained
at www.ICGtesting.com
Printed in the USA
BVHW092110120520
578662BV00001B/4

9 781612 448404